Made in the USA
Middletown, DE
10 May 2022

65587717R00068